True Tales of t

Qui...
Gu...

Jeff Savage

Enslow Publishers, Inc.
40 Industrial Road
Box 398
Berkeley Heights, NJ 07922
USA

http://www.enslow.com

Original edition published as *Gunfighters of the Wild West* in 1995.

Library of Congress Cataloging-in-Publication Data
Savage, Jeff, 1961–
  Quick-draw gunfighters : true tales of the Wild West / Jeff Savage.
    p. cm. — (True tales of the Wild West)
  Rev. ed. of: Gunfighters of the Wild West. 1995.
  Includes bibliographical references and index.
  Summary: "Examines gunfighters in the Wild West, including the typical traits and tools of gunfighters, infamous outlaws, gangs, important lawmen, and how the gun often ruled the Wild West"—Provided by publisher.
  ISBN 978-0-7660-4021-2
  1. Outlaws—West (U.S.)—History—Juvenile literature. 2. Peace officers—West (U.S.)—History—Juvenile literature. 3. West (U.S.)—History—Juvenile literature. I. Savage, Jeff, 1961– Gunfighters of the Wild West. II. Title.
  F596.S2354 2012
  364.1092'2—dc23
                        2011028121

Paperback ISBN 978-1-4644-0029-2

ePUB ISBN 978-1-4645-0479-2

PDF ISBN 978-1-4646-0479-9

Printed in the United States of America

092011 Lake Book Manufacturing, Inc., Melrose Park, IL

10 9 8 7 6 5 4 3 2 1

To Our Readers: We have done our best to make sure all Internet addresses in this book were active and appropriate when we went to press. However, the author and the Publisher have no control over, and assume no liability for, the material available on those Internet sites or on other Web sites they may link to. Any comments or suggestions can be sent by e-mail to comments@enslow.com or to the address on the back cover.

♻ Enslow Publishers, Inc., is committed to printing our books on recycled paper. The paper in every book contains 10% to 30% post-consumer waste (PCW). The cover board on the outside of each book contains 100% PCW. Our goal is to do our part to help young people and the environment too!

Illustration Credits: Denver Public Library, Western History / Genealogy Department, p. 10; © Enslow Publishers, Inc. / Paul Daly, p. 1; Everett Collection, p. 22; Kansas State Historical Society, p. 14; Library of Congress Prints and Photographs, pp. 18, 26, 32; Mary Evans Picture Library / Everett Collection, p. 13; Courtesy Mercaldo Archives, from *Dictionary of American Portraits*, Dover Publications, Inc., 1967, p. 40; © 2011 Photos.com, a division of Getty Images, p. 37; © 20th Century Fox Film Corp. / Everett Collection, p. 43.

Cover Illustration: © Enslow Publishers, Inc. / Paul Daly.

Contents

Chapter 1
The O.K. Corral 5

Chapter 2
The Gunfighter 11

Chapter 3
The Outlaws 17

Chapter 4
The Gangs 25

Chapter 5
The Lawmen 34

Chapter 6
The End of the Gunfighter 41

Chapter Notes 45

Glossary 46

Further Reading
(Books and Internet Addresses) 47

Index 48

chapter 1

The O.K. Corral

The four notorious men walked slowly down Fourth Street. They were dressed in black. Each was carrying a gun. They were Doc Holliday and the Earp brothers—Wyatt, Morgan, and Virgil. They were out for blood.

Around the corner, on Fremont Street, four other men were waiting for them. They were the Clanton brothers and the McLaury brothers. They also had guns. It looked like terrible trouble.

It was a cold, blustery day in Tombstone, Arizona, on October 26, 1881. Ike and Billy Clanton, with Tom and Frank McLaury, had ridden horses into town to drink in the saloons. Virgil Earp was the city marshal of Tombstone, and he and his brothers didn't care much for rowdy cowboys like the Clantons and the McLaurys. Morgan Earp didn't appreciate it a month earlier when Frank McLaury challenged him to step into the middle of the street to fight. Five months before that, Wyatt Earp caught Billy Clanton in the saddle of his stolen horse. Each time, the Earps could have fought. Instead, they kept their cool.

It would be different this time. Ike Clanton, who did most of his fighting with his mouth, was drinking shots of whiskey in the Alhambra Saloon. He hated the Earps, and he claimed that Tombstone would be a better town without them in it. Doc Holliday, a friend of the Earps, overheard Ike's boasting. Holliday swore at Ike, then challenged him to a shooting match. Ike backed down.

Virgil Earp's responsibility as city marshal was to keep the peace; Wyatt and Morgan served as his assistants. When Virgil heard that Ike Clanton was threatening the Earps, he went out to find him. Virgil spotted Ike in an alley, approached him from behind, and grabbed his rifle. Ike tried to draw his six-shooter, but Virgil hit him over the head with a revolver. Then he arrested Ike for carrying guns within city limits.

Ike was wiping blood from his head when Wyatt Earp found him outside the courthouse a short time later. "You've threatened my life two or three times," Wyatt said. "I want this thing stopped."

Ike muttered a few words.

"You . . . dirty cow thief," Wyatt said. "If you're anxious to fight, I'll meet you."

"I'll see you after I get through here," Ike answered, as he stepped into the courthouse.[1]

Later that day, Cochise County sheriff John Behan was getting a shave in a barbershop when he noticed a crowd gathering on the corner. The barber said it looked like trouble, and Sheriff Behan hurried outside.

The Earp brothers were marching down Fourth Street. Because he was the marshal, it was Virgil's duty to disarm the cowboys. Sheriff Behan was a friend of the cowboys, mostly because he needed cowboy votes to be reelected sheriff. Sheriff Behan asked the Earps to hold on a minute. The sheriff said he would get the Clantons and McLaurys to give up their guns. The Earps agreed to wait. Sheriff Behan disappeared around the corner.

The Clantons and McLaurys were huddled around the corner on Fremont Street. Billy Clanton, Ike's little brother, didn't want to fight in the first place. He was mad at Ike for being such a loudmouth, but he had to stand beside his brother.

"Boys, you must give me your arms," Sheriff Behan said.[2]

The Clantons and McLaurys refused. The Earps resumed their march. Doc Holliday ran up from behind. The Earps were his best friends; he insisted on helping. Virgil accepted Holliday's help. He temporarily deputized Holliday right there in the street. Then Virgil handed Holliday a shotgun.

Holliday and the Earps turned the corner. They peered down Fremont Street and spotted the Clantons and McLaurys on the sidewalk next to the O.K. Corral. Sheriff Behan came running up to Virgil. He pleaded with Virgil not to go down there. The Earps didn't listen. They headed toward the cowboys.

A crowd looked on as Doc Holliday and the Earps reached the Clantons and McLaurys. The two groups stood less than ten feet apart. They stared each other down. The silence was broken with a *click, click,* as Billy Clanton and Frank McLaury cocked their six-shooters. Somebody yelled, and the shoot-out began.

After the first shot was fired, Ike Clanton tossed away his pistol and ran up to Wyatt Earp. Ike begged Wyatt not to shoot him. Wyatt told Ike to fight or clear out. Ike ran away down the street.

Wyatt pulled a six-shooter out of his coat pocket and shot Frank McLaury in the stomach. Frank, wounded badly, stumbled into the street. Billy Clanton aimed his pistol at Wyatt, but before he could shoot, Morgan Earp fired a bullet through Billy's chest. Earp shot Billy again, in the wrist and stomach. Billy slumped to the ground.

Tom McLaury had been hiding behind a horse, but the horse bolted into the street. Doc Holliday took aim with the shotgun, and he blasted buckshot into Tom's right side. Tom staggered down Fremont Street to the corner where he collapsed, dead.

Virgil Earp had not fired a shot. Suddenly, he felt a bullet tear into his leg. Billy Clanton was on the ground, bleeding but still shooting. Billy fired again, and this time a bullet ripped into Morgan Earp's shoulder. Morgan and Wyatt turned toward Billy and shot together—and Billy was dead.

Frank McLaury clutched his stomach and fired once more from the street. The shot struck Doc Holliday's holster, then grazed his side. Morgan Earp took aim, and he shot Frank just below the right ear.

The shoot-out was over. It had lasted less than a minute. Three men were dead, and three more were wounded. The three dead cowboys were displayed in caskets behind a storefront window, under a sign that said: MURDERED IN THE STREETS OF TOMBSTONE. They were later buried at Boot Hill.

The gunfight in Tombstone, Arizona, on October 26, 1881, ended bloodily, with three men dead and three wounded. The bodies of the dead were displayed in a storefront window. Pictured here from left are the bodies of Billy Clanton, Frank McLaury, and Tom McLaury.

Holliday and the Earp brothers were put on trial for murder. The trial lasted a month, and the defendants were declared not guilty. That didn't keep friends of the cowboys from seeking revenge. Two months after the gunfight, Marshal Virgil Earp was ambushed in the dark by unseen assailants in front of the Cosmopolitan Hotel. His left arm was shattered forever. He tried to console his wife by saying, "Never mind. I've got one arm left to hug you with."[3]

chapter 2

The Gunfighter

Gunfighters in the Wild West were a flashy, self-confident breed. They did not try to avoid trouble—they *looked* for it. They considered gunfighting to be an art, like painting or writing poetry.

There were two distinct classes of gunfighters: outlaws and lawmen. They often squared off against one another—outlaws on the side of wrong, lawmen on the side of right. Whichever side of the law they were on, the gun was their most prized possession.

Reputation

Whether they were good or bad at heart, all gunfighters had one thing in common: They were feared and famous. Gunfighters seemed to command a certain respect from the average townsfolk. Everyone knew of men like Tulsa Jack Blake, Bully Brooks, Dynamite Dick Clifton, Flat Nose Curry, and Turkey Creek Jack Johnson.

Most gunfighters enjoyed their reputations. It made them feel powerful when men would clear out of the way as they rode through town on their horses or walked through a saloon to the bar.

When these gunfighters would get drunk, they would boast about how many men they had killed, or, even worse, how many they *planned* to kill. Some liked to exaggerate. Wild Bill Hickok, for instance, once bragged to a reporter that he had killed more than one hundred men. This is known to be a wild lie.

Not all gunfighters bragged, however. There was one spectacular shoot-out in Newton, Kansas, in 1871; the hero of that story was never found. A pack of cowboys came rushing into a dance hall with guns blazing. Out of nowhere, a thin boy jumped in front of them and fired away, killing four of the cowboys. When the smoke cleared, the boy could not be found. No one knew anything about him, except that his name was James Riley and that he was dying of tuberculosis.

Gunfighters had to uphold their reputations. If challenged in a saloon, during a poker game, or on the street, a gunfighter had to be ready. Any gunfighter who backed down from a challenge was considered a coward.

When outlaws attempted bank robberies, shoot-outs usually ensued. This photo shows bullet holes in the windows of a bank in Coffeyville, Kansas, after an unsuccessful robbery attempt by the Dalton brothers on October 5, 1892.

The Quick Draw

Gunfighters knew that if they made one mistake, they wouldn't get a chance to make another, so they spent long hours practicing the art of handling guns. The most common gunfighting technique was that of drawing the six-shooter from the holster. Gunmen tirelessly rehearsed the movement—reach and draw, reach and draw—until they could draw, cock, and fire all in one smooth lightning-quick movement.

The legendary gunfight in the Wild West was the duel. In reality, it wasn't a common practice, simply because most shootings ended swiftly, often with one cowardly man shooting another in the back. The duel was thought to be the fairest way to settle a dispute, though. Opponents would stand back-to-back with guns drawn. They would carefully step a set number of paces away from each other. Then they would turn and fire. Sometimes they wouldn't even bother with the steps. They would just meet in the street a distance away and stare each other down, each waiting for the other to reach for his gun. Either way, the man left standing would live to see another day—probably not for long, though. Gunfighting was a hazardous affair.

There were two sure places in the Wild West where you could find gunfighters—saloons and banks. Fights usually erupted in saloons when men drank too much liquor. These brawls often involved punches, kicks, and sometimes a few thrown bottles, or broken chairs—not much more.

Bank Robbing

Banks were a different story. Outlaws robbed banks with guns; shoot-outs resulted. People were killed, and only the best gunmen survived.

Some gunfighters considered it a challenge to rob a bank. Henry Starr, one of the last outlaws to do his robbing while seated on a horse, told a reporter for the *St. Louis Globe* about the thrill of bank robbery:

> It isn't only the lure of money that takes a man into outlawry. There's the thrill of dashing into a town after an all-night ride, guns blazing. From every window across the street, rifles and shotguns are spitting lead at you. The boys who had gone into the bank run out with a grain sack bulging with loot. It's time to leave. One of your boys is down, stretched out in the dust. You realize there is nothing you can do for him. You vault into the saddle and roar out of town, guns bucking. You think of the boy you left lying back there in the dust. It's tough, but you realize that it may be you the next time.[1]

chapter 3

The Outlaws

Some men weren't satisfied with earning a decent living. They imagined having riches and fame. They figured that being quick on the draw gave them the right to take anything they wanted. So they became outlaws.

Outlaws came from all sorts of backgrounds. Some had been on the run from the law ever since they were children. Others learned to handle a gun fighting in the Civil War. Some had been upstanding individuals in the community before turning bad. A few even wised up later in life to become decent citizens, or even lawmen. A few were wealthy, but most were poor. A few were along in years when they turned bad, but most were just youths when they began a life of crime. A few were educated, but most were quite ignorant.

Cole Younger was a ruthless outlaw and a member of the James gang.

Nearly all outlaws shared one common trait—they did not obey the law of mutual respect. They thought, wrongly, that they were more important than anyone else. Their friends were afraid to challenge them for fear of getting hurt or killed. So they rode along, shooting and hurting people, until they wound up in prison—or dead.

The Cruelty of Outlaws

The behavior of some of the outlaws who roamed the Wild West was downright cruel. Bill Longley once shot a man to death in a camp because he thought the man was looking at him while he tried to sleep. John Wesley Hardin is said to have killed forty-four men in ten years. In one of his first killings, when he was fifteen years old, Hardin drilled three bullets through his cousin after an argument.

Who could forget the notorious Cole Younger, who eventually joined the James Gang? Legend has it that during the Civil War, Cole tested a rifle by firing it into the backs of several Union prisoners tied together and stacked against a tree. He wanted to see how many bodies one bullet would go through.

Clay Allison

One of the most notorious outlaws was sharpshooter Clay Allison. He was considered insane by many, though no one dared tell him so to his face. Among Allison's favorite hobbies was riding stark naked up and down the street on his white horse, then inviting flabbergasted citizens to the saloon for a drink.

Allison once broke into a jail with a mob and lynched an accused murderer. Allison then cut off the dead man's head and placed it on a pole in a saloon.

Allison often drew his gun and shot at anything or anybody. One evening, he was shooting the lights out of a saloon in New Mexico when the town marshal approached him. The marshal asked Allison kindly to stop, and Allison wheeled around and shot him. Another time, when Allison and his brother entered a dance hall, the marshal asked them to remove their guns. Allison fired bullets through the marshal's heart.

Even when Allison wasn't shooting people, he was wreaking other kinds of havoc. A dentist once drilled the wrong tooth in Allison's mouth. Allison went off angrily to another dentist to have the procedure done right. He later returned to the first dentist. The outlaw grabbed the dentist, pinned him to the chair, and yanked out a couple of the dentist's teeth—without administering an anesthetic.

John King Fisher

Many outlaws were ruthless. A Texan named John King Fisher once shot a man through the head, apparently for no reason. People joked that Fisher wanted to see if the bullet would bounce off the man's bald head. Fisher was arrested for this crime, and for several others, through the course of his evil young life. But he was never held in jail for long. Sometimes the prosecution could find no witnesses, usually because citizens were afraid to testify against Fisher. Sometimes Fisher was released from jail early because of overcrowding.

Shortly after being released from the Texas state penitentiary in 1871, Fisher teamed up with a group of Mexican cattle rustlers. While splitting up the money following the sale of stolen cattle, Fisher shot three of the Mexicans dead. He then took control of the rustling operation and was reputed to have killed several more men while selling stolen Texas cattle across the border in Mexico.

Fisher befriended another notorious outlaw, Ben Thompson, who had many enemies in San Antonio, Texas. When the two outlaws entered that town one day, Fisher's friend was gunned down—and so was Fisher. He was found dead with thirteen bullets in him.

Billy the Kid

Perhaps the most famous outlaw of all was Henry McCarty. At some point he took the name William H. Bonney. But he is known best as Billy the Kid. Billy had his first brush with the law in the town of Silver City, New Mexico, when he was fifteen. Billy took part in a practical joke by hiding a bundle of clothes from a Chinese laundryman. He was caught and tossed in the local jail to learn a lesson. After sitting still for two days, Billy could stand it no longer; he escaped by climbing up the chimney. He didn't stop running until he reached Arizona. Billy had become a fugitive.

A wealthy New Mexico cattleman and banker named John Tunstall eventually befriended Billy. The young outlaw had no parents, and he thought of John Tunstall as a father. At the time, rival merchants and

REWARD

($5,000.00)

Reward for the capture, dead or alive, of one Wm. Wright, better known as

"BILLY THE KID"

Age, 18. Height, 5 feet, 3 inches. Weight, 125 lbs. Light hair, blue eyes and even features. He is the leader of the worst band of desperadoes the Territory has ever had to deal with. The above reward will be paid for his capture or positive proof of his death.

JIM DALTON, Sheriff.

DEAD OR ALIVE!
"BILLY THE KID"

One of the most well-known outlaws in American history, Billy the Kid had lawmen tracking him all over the New Mexico Territory. This "reward" poster offered $5,000 for his capture or death.

ranchers were caught up in a feud known as the Lincoln County War.

When a rival posse showed up one day to steal Tunstall's horses, Tunstall protested. He was shot in the head. Billy was standing nearby when his boss was gunned down. He couldn't believe his eyes. He did not give chase because he was hopelessly outnumbered, but Billy pledged to avenge Tunstall's murder.

He searched for Tunstall's killers with a group that called itself the Regulators. Billy's group found two of the killers in the countryside. The two men surrendered with the promise of being returned to the town of Lincoln alive. On the way back to Lincoln, Billy pulled out his rifle and shot them both dead. Then he gunned down one of the Regulators, who had tried to protect them. A few days later, Billy encountered Sheriff William Brady and his deputies. Shooting from behind a stone wall, Billy killed the sheriff and one of the deputies.

By now, Billy was being tracked all over New Mexico. He became famous for his amazing escapes from the law. One time, he was captured and thrown in jail, with iron cuffs around his wrists and feet. He was sentenced to death. Two weeks before the execution, the Kid somehow managed to kill both guards and break free. There was just no holding Billy the Kid.

On July 13, 1881, time ran out on Billy. Sheriff Pat Garrett rode to Fort Sumner after learning that Billy was hiding nearby. The sheriff went to the home of an old friend named Pete Maxwell. It was midnight, and Billy was visiting a young Mexican woman in a building on Maxwell's ranch. Sheriff Garrett went into Maxwell's bedroom to wake the rancher. At that moment, Billy walked across the yard to Maxwell's house to get something to eat. When Billy saw a strange horse tied up outside, he went in to see Maxwell. He stepped inside Maxwell's bedroom.

The room was dark, and Billy could not see well. He said, "Who are they, Pete?" Sheriff Garrett was sitting on the edge of the bed. Maxwell whispered to the sheriff, "That's him."[1] Billy knew someone else was in the room, and he yelled in Spanish, "Quién es? Quién es?" ("Who is it? Who is it?")[2]

Right then, Sheriff Garrett jumped up with his pistol and fired a shot at Billy. The bullet pierced Billy's heart. Garrett dived to the floor and shot again. This time he missed, but it didn't matter. Billy fell to the floor, gasping for air. In another minute, Billy the Kid was dead.

chapter 4

The Gangs

Most outlaws probably realized that they would someday meet their match. Whether it was death in a gunfight by a quicker-drawing foe or a bullet to the back of the head, outlaws were sure to get it as long as they stayed criminals.

A few outlaws wised up and went straight. Many, however, sought protection by joining forces with other outlaws. The more guns on their side, they figured, the better their chances of shooting their way out of trouble. The outlaws would have to split the loot with their partners. Although that was better than the alternative—death.

These groups formed by outlaws were called gangs, and among the gangs of the Wild West were some of the most fearsome gunfighters alive.

This portrait of Jesse James was taken around 1864. The James Gang robbed banks and trains in several states.

A favorite target of outlaw gangs was the town bank. It was where most of the citizens kept their money, and it was usually well guarded. When the robbery was over, a gang's gunfighting work had just begun. Lawmen and citizens alike usually tried to shoot the robbers. If the gang escaped out of town, a posse often formed to chase after them. The robbers needed great sharpshooting skills, as well as a little luck, to fight off the pursuers.

Gangs weren't satisfied with robbing only banks. They robbed trains, stagecoaches, and ranches, too. Wherever money or horses or cattle could be stolen, gangs usually lurked nearby.

The James Gang

No gang had a more notorious reputation than the James Gang, led by Jesse and his brother, Frank.

The James Gang rode high for fifteen years, making at least twenty-six big robberies.

It all began for the James Gang on a February afternoon in 1866. A dozen men rode into Liberty, Missouri. They stopped in front of the Clay County Savings Association bank; two of them went inside. One of the men walked up to a bank teller and took out a six-shooter. He demanded all the money in the bank. It was a strange request; an American bank had never been robbed before in broad daylight. The two men hurdled over the counter and pointed their guns at the bank teller. The teller hurried to the vault, opened it, and poured into a sack all the gold, silver coins, and dollar bills the sack could hold. The two robbers dashed out of the bank with the loot. They mounted their horses and galloped down the street.

A nineteen-year-old college student was on his way to class when he saw the riders coming. He ran to take cover, but it was too late. One robber fired his gun four times at the student, killing him instantly. Later, it was discovered that any one of the four bullets would have been fatal. A posse chased after the gang, but they never did find it. The James Gang made off with about $60,000. The state of Missouri knew it had some real trouble on its hands.

The James Gang began robbing trains, too. Bankers and train conductors became so desperate that they hired the famous Pinkerton's National Detective Agency to hunt down the James Gang. The detective agency's symbol was an open eye, with the slogan "We never sleep." It is considered the origin of the term "private eye."

When it was learned that several members of the James Gang were hiding out at a farm near Liberty, Missouri, a Pinkerton agent set out for the farm. The agent's body was found near the farm the next day, shot through the head and heart.[1]

The James Gang finally met its match in Minnesota. The townsfolk of Northfield foiled a bank robbery by killing two members of the gang and wounding several others. A posse hunted down the rest of the gang. Only Jesse and Frank escaped.

The end came for Jesse James on April 3, 1882, at his home in St. Joseph, Missouri. After breakfast, Jesse went into the living room with Charlie and Bob Ford, a pair of brothers who were pretending to help Jesse plan a bank robbery. Really, the Ford brothers were after the reward money that came with capturing or killing Jesse James. James stepped up on a chair to straighten a picture on the wall. Bob quickly drew his pistol and fired a shot into the back of James's head. Jesse collapsed and died instantly. The days of the James Gang finally were over.

Several other gangs tried to imitate the James Gang—and some proved nearly as notorious.

The Daltons

The Dalton brothers—Emmett, Grattan, and Bob— were sharpshooters who grew up near Coffeyville, Kansas. They were cousins of the Youngers. The Dalton Gang gained some attention in 1890 for robbing trains, but they weren't recognized as the ruthless outlaws that their cousins were. This bothered the Dalton brothers; they wanted to be famous and feared. This desire proved to be their downfall.

The Daltons met their doom in their hometown of Coffeyville when they tried to rob two banks at once in 1892. They rode into town disguised in fake beards and mustaches, but townspeople recognized them anyway. They also picked a bad time to pull off the heist. The street in front of the two banks was under repair, and the robbers had to leave their horses a block away and walk to the banks on foot.

As the Daltons approached the banks, citizens ran home to get their guns. Merchants passed out firearms to everyone around. The gang managed to seize $20,000 from one of the banks, but they struck out at the second bank when the teller convinced them that the vault had a time lock and could not be opened. The whole town was armed when the Daltons charged out of the banks. A horrendous battle ensued. The gang killed four citizens in the gunfight. All members of the gang, except Emmett, were also killed. Emmett served fifteen years in prison.

The Doolin Gang

The Doolin Gang was a dastardly band of ten men who killed many people while robbing banks and trains across the Wild West. Bill Doolin organized the gang in 1892, and its reign of terror lasted three years, until most of its members had been gunned down.

The Doolin Gang staged carefully planned robberies in an effort to avoid disaster. Still, it seemed that each heist resulted in the loss of one or more members. After a bank in Oklahoma was looted, Crescent Sam Yountis was tracked down by lawmen and shot dead before he could spend any of his $4,500 share of the money. Then a double train holdup resulted in the loss of Arkansas Tom Jones.

Another train heist led to the death of Tulsa Jack Blake and the expulsion from the gang of Red Buck Waightman, for crazy gunplay. Two more members were killed by gunfire during the holdup of an express office. By then the gang was too small to survive. Bill Doolin returned home to his wife; he died a year later from a lung disease.

The Wild Bunch

One gang that may never have been stopped was the Wild Bunch, led by Butch Cassidy and the Sundance Kid. It is rumored that Cassidy and Sundance were killed in a gun battle with troops in South America. A more popular belief, though, is that Cassidy died of old age in the United States. Either way, their robberies are legendary.

The Wild Bunch robbed everything—banks, trains, mining camps, and ranches. Butch tried his best not to kill anyone, though. When his gang was pursued by posses, Cassidy always shot at the horse, not the rider.

Harry "Sundance Kid" Longabaugh was Cassidy's partner. Longabaugh was nicknamed the Sundance Kid because he served eighteen months in jail when he was a boy for stealing a horse in Sundance, Wyoming.

The fate of Butch Cassidy and the Sundance Kid is unknown. Some people believe that they fled to South America, along with Sundance's sweetheart, Etta Place, where they were killed. This portrait of the Sundance Kid and Etta was taken around 1900.

Some people say the Sundance Kid was the best sharpshooter in the world.

Butch Cassidy and the Sundance Kid became famous for robbing trains by blowing up their safes with dynamite. They pulled their first heist on the morning of June 2, 1899. They stopped a train on the Union-Pacific Railroad in Wyoming by flashing a phony warning lantern. Before the conductor knew what was going on, Butch and Sundance disconnected the express car that held the safe. They explained to the guard in the express car that they were going to blow open the car. The stubborn guard refused to leave the express car. So, instead of using two or three sticks of dynamite, they used only one stick, hoping not to injure the guard. The car door blew open, and the guard staggered out, dazed but not hurt. The Wild Bunch used a second stick of dynamite to blow open the safe. Dollar bills flew everywhere. The gang gathered up about $30,000 worth of currency and then rode off to safety.

They robbed several more trains in the same manner. After many years of such daring tactics, the two outlaws, along with Sundance's sweetheart, Etta Place, fled to South America, where they may have met their fate.

chapter 5

The Lawmen

With so many robbers, desperadoes, and gangs on the loose, good citizens were desperate for law and order. They hired men adept with guns to keep the peace. These were the lawmen.

It was the responsibility of the lawman to head off trouble before it began. When shady characters rode into town, the lawman kept an eye on them. Sometimes he asked them to give up their guns. Sometimes he asked them to clear out of town.

Lawmen had a dangerous job. Whether they were marshals, sheriffs, or rangers, they had to stand tall against all enemies. If a gang of sharpshooters rode into town looking for trouble, a lawman would try to rustle up some help from the local citizens. He would deputize men on the spot and hand them weapons.

When he couldn't find help, he would have to face the gang alone. It was a good thing that some of the best gunfighters in the Wild West were the men who wore the lawman's badge.

Wild Bill Hickok

Perhaps the most celebrated lawman ever was James Butler "Wild Bill" Hickok. Hickok happened to be in Hays City, Kansas, when citizens there demanded law and order. George A. Custer, a lieutenant colonel at nearby Fort Hays and a Civil War hero, knew of Hickok's exploits as an army scout. Custer suggested his friend Hickok for the job. The citizens knew of Hickok's reputation, but they decided to take a chance anyway, and they appointed him town marshal. The longhaired Hickok took an instant liking to being on the right side of the law. In a saloon, he killed two men who foolishly drew their pistols on him. He killed a third man—who happened to be his archenemy—when the man tried to outshoot him.

Wild Bill left Hays City after a skirmish in another saloon with members of the U.S. Seventh Cavalry. There is debate over exactly what happened. One version has it that Wild Bill was standing with his back to a group of approaching cavalrymen when suddenly he drew both his six-shooters, firing one over his shoulder and the other to his side, killing two men. Friends smuggled him aboard the next train out of town. When asked later why he fled Hays City, Hickok replied, "I couldn't fight the whole Seventh Cavalry."[1]

Hickok later surfaced in Abilene, Kansas, where he was named marshal. Hickok was a gambler, and he spent most of his time at the poker table. Anyone who needed the town marshal would go to the Alamo Saloon, where Hickok played cards.

Wild Bill went too far with his gunplay one day when he fired a barrage of shots into a group of squabbling drunks, killing one of them, and a police-man as well. Hickok resigned immediately, and for a few years he became a drifter. He was killed five years later when a man sneaked up behind him at a poker table and shot him in the back of the head.

Henry Brown

Other towns were having trouble finding and keeping reliable lawmen. In Caldwell, Kansas, three different town marshals were gunned down within one year. Citizens were desperate. One day, a short, blue-eyed man named Henry Brown rode into Caldwell, packing two six-shooters and a Winchester rifle. Brown went

Wild Bill Hickok had to resign as marshal in Abilene, Kansas, after shooting into a crowd of fighting drunks, killing two people. He never regained his post as a lawman and was murdered at a poker table.

to the mayor's office to ask for a lawman's job. "All right," the mayor was reported to have said. "It's your funeral."[2] Brown was named assistant marshal. No one realized Henry Brown was one of the most famous desperadoes of the Southwest.

He did such a good job keeping the peace that he was promoted to head marshal within six months.

He demonstrated his shooting skills when he killed a man resisting arrest and when he killed a gambler who tried to outshoot him. Brown's deputy was a big Texan named Ben Wheeler. Together, they walked down the streets of Caldwell, toting their guns in the name of law and order.

Henry did not drink, gamble, or smoke. He represented the good, clean image of a lawman. The citizens of Caldwell presented him with a gift of appreciation—a shiny, new Winchester rifle. Brown married a town girl and bought a house. Then, without warning, Brown turned outlaw again. He rode out of town with Ben Wheeler, and they met two more men on the trail. The four men rode to a small town, where they tried to rob a bank. They shot and killed the bank teller, wounded the president, and were soon being chased out of town by a posse. They were cornered in a canyon, captured, and hauled back to town, where they were thrown in jail.

That night, an angry mob broke into the jail, overpowered the sheriff, and charged after Brown and his group. Brown made a run for it and was riddled with bullets. He died instantly. The other three men were dragged to the edge of town and hanged. The citizens of Caldwell were stunned and saddened.

Ben Thompson

Ben Thompson was marshal of Austin, Texas. He policed his town with the same kind of grit as did Henry Brown in Caldwell. Thompson was a celebrated gunfighter who fought for the Confederate army in the Civil War, and for Emperor Maximilian's forces in Mexico. Bat Masterson, another lawman, wrote that Ben was "the most dangerous killer in the Old West."[3]

Thompson admitted to killing at least thirty-two men. His presence in Austin made rowdies think twice about causing trouble. Thompson would sometimes get drunk and shoot out the street lamps. The citizens of Austin seemed to put up with this behavior. They were happy to have such a fearsome gunfighter looking out for them.

Bat Masterson

Bat Masterson also was appreciated while serving as a lawman in Kansas. One terrible night, he was attacked in a saloon by a group of soldiers and was shot in the hip. Masterson would have been killed that night, but Ben Thompson came to his rescue. He challenged the soldiers with his six-shooters. For the rest of his life, Masterson walked with the aid of a cane.

Although Bat Masterson had a quick draw and great aim, he did not rely on his guns. He liked to whack lawbreakers with his cane.

Masterson served as a deputy marshal in Dodge City with his friend Wyatt Earp. Masterson later became sheriff of Ford County, Kansas. He was a quick shooter with deadeye aim, but he seldom used his guns. Most times, Masterson took care of trouble by whacking the troublemakers with his cane.

As feared as some lawmen were on the frontier, there never seemed to be enough of them to keep the peace. There were too many gunslingers on the loose.

chapter 6

The End of the Gunfighter

Although the legends don't say so, the life of the gunfighter was usually quite lonely. Gunfighters were always on the move, forever searching for something bigger and better. Most never found what they were looking for. Instead, their lives were almost always cut short by the very tool of their trade—the gun.

Gunfighters in the Wild West lived in fear of dying without their boots on. Many did, and early in life. Few gunslingers lived past their thirties. Many other gunfighters simply disappeared without a trace.

The Taming of the West

Towns grew, and the wide open Wild West became more populous. Citizens insisted on law and order. More lawmen were hired to keep the peace, making it more difficult for desperadoes to shoot their way out of trouble. The mere presence of peace officers made outlaws think twice about causing trouble.

Using modern technology rather than guns made tracking outlaws easier. With the telegraph and later the telephone, lawmen informed one another of the whereabouts of dangerous gunslingers. Loading their horses onto trains, peace officers and posses could speed ahead in the direction that the outlaws were fleeing. The posses would greet the outlaws at their final destination. The lawmen would use the horses for the last miles of the chase. If the chase ended in a deadly gunfight, photographs were taken of the outlaws who were gunned down. It was thought that a picture of a man riddled with bullet holes would prevent future gunfights.

Captured murderers were usually sentenced to death. Public hangings were held in town squares to further discourage would-be outlaws. A double hanging of murderers in Leadville, Colorado, for instance, drew a crowd of ten thousand citizens. The townsfolk hoped that children who witnessed a man hanging from a rope might be less inclined to become bank robbers or murderers.

Gunfighters in the Wild West—both outlaws and lawmen—became legendary figures, often portrayed in books, plays, television, and movies. Actors Paul Newman (left) and Robert Redford famously played the Wild Bunch outlaws in the 1969 film *Butch Cassidy and the Sundance Kid*.

Fade-out

Eventually, this violent breed of men began to fade from society. By the turn of the century, gunslingers galloping into town with guns blazing were a rare sight. The most hardened criminals committed crimes until they were either killed or jailed. Many lawmen were killed in the line of duty.

Those lawmen and outlaws who did survive the dangers of living by their guns eventually hung them up. Some got ordinary jobs, some turned bad, and some, like Wyatt Earp, never really settled down. Until his death in 1929 at the age of eighty, Earp dreamed of finding a big mining stake.

Earp's friend Bat Masterson gave up his lawman's badge, moved to New York, and became a sportswriter. He died, aged sixty-eight, at his desk in the *Morning Telegraph* newspaper office.

Not only lawmen lived on to old age. Emmett Dalton survived the disastrous 1892 Coffeyville bank robbery. After serving a fifteen-year sentence, he went straight. In 1920, Dalton moved to Los Angeles, where he wrote movie scripts and appeared in a few movies. He died in 1937.

Chapter Notes

Chapter 1. The O.K. Corral

1. Casey Tefertiller, "Wyatt Earp's Last Stand," *San Francisco Examiner* (October 17, 1993), pp. 14–19.
2. Paul Trachtman, *The Gunfighters* (Alexandria, Va.: Time-Life Books, 1974), p. 27.
3. Ibid., p. 34.

Chapter 2. The Gunfighter

1. Harry Sinclair Drago, *The Legend Makers* (Cornwall, N.Y.: Cornwall Press, Inc., 1975), p. vi.

Chapter 3. The Outlaws

1. Paul Trachtman, *The Gunfighters* (Alexandria, Va.: Time-Life Books, 1974), p. 190.
2. Jay Robert Nash, *Encyclopedia of Western Lawmen & Outlaws* (New York: Paragon House, 1989), p. 44.

Chapter 4. The Gangs

1. Paul Trachtman, *The Gunfighters* (Alexandria, Va.: Time-Life Books, 1974), p. 68.

Chapter 5. The Lawmen

1. Harry Sinclair Drago, *The Legend Makers* (Cornwall, N.Y.: Cornwall Press, Inc., 1975), p. 26.
2. Paul Trachtman, *The Gunfighters* (Alexandria, Va.: Time-Life Books, 1974), p. 110.
3. W. B. (Bat) Masterson, *Famous Gun Fighters of the Western Frontier* (Monroe, Wash.: Weatherford Press, 1982), p. 38.

Glossary

anesthetic—A painkiller given by doctors and dentists to patients having surgery.

buckshot—Lead bullets fired from a shotgun.

cavalry—A group of army men mounted on horses.

deputize—To make an ordinary person an officer of the law for a short time. In the Wild West, lawmen sometimes needed extra help from citizens to fight outlaws.

desperadoes—Violent, ruthless criminals.

duel—A type of gunfight in which opponents stand back to back, walk a certain number of steps apart, and then turn and fire.

heist—An armed robbery.

marshal—The head lawman of a town.

posse—A group of people who travel together for some common purpose, usually to capture criminals trying to escape.

rustlers—Cattle thieves.

saloons—Places where people could play cards and drink whiskey in the frontier towns of the Wild West.

sheriff—In the Wild West, the chief law officer of a county.

shotgun—A type of gun that is fired from the shoulder.

six-shooter—A revolver with chambers for six bullets.

telegraph—A system of wires that made it possible for people to send messages across long distances.

Further Reading

Books

Bard, Jessica. *Lawmen and Outlaws: The Wild, Wild West.* New York: Children's Press, 2005.

McIntosh, Kenneth. *Saloons, Shootouts, and Spurs: The Wild West in the 1800s.* Broomall, Pa.: Mason Crest Publishers, 2011.

Nelson, Vaunda Micheaux. *Bad News for Outlaws: The Remarkable Life of Bass Reeves, Deputy U.S. Marshal.* Minneapolis, Minn.: Carolrhoda Books, 2009.

Robinson, J. Dennis. *Jesse James: Legendary Rebel and Outlaw.* Mankato, Minn.: Compass Point Books, 2007.

Stefoff, Rebecca. *The Wild West.* New York: Marshall Cavendish Benchmark, 2007.

Internet Addresses

Legends of America: Outlaws, Gunfighters, Lawmen & More
<http://www.legendsofamerica.com/we-outlawsandlegends.html>

Old West Kansas: Gunfighters, Outlaws, and Lawmen
<http://www.vlib.us/old_west/guns.html>

The Wild West Outlaws and Lawmen
<http://www.thewildwest.org/cowboys/wildwestoutlawsandlawmen>

Index

A

Allison, Clay, 19–20

B

bank robbery, 15–16,
26, 27, 29–30
Behan, John, 7, 8
Blake, Tulsa Jack,
12, 31
bragging, 12
Brown, Henry, 36–38

C

Cassidy, Butch, 31–33
Clanton, Ike/Billy,
5–10
cruelty, 18–19
Custer, George A., 35

D

Dalton, Emmett, 29, 44
Dalton gang, 29–30
Doolin, Bill, 30, 31
Doolin Gang, 30–31
duels, 15

E

Earp, Morgan, 5–10
Earp, Virgil, 5–10
Earp, Wyatt, 5–10,
40, 44

F

Fisher, John King,
20–21

G

gangs, 25–26
Garrett, Pat, 24

gunfighters generally,
11–16, 41–44

H

Hardin, John Wesley,
18
Hickok, Wild Bill, 12,
35–36
Holliday, Doc, 5–10

J

James, Jesse/Frank,
26–29
James Gang, 26–29
Jones, Arkansas
Tom, 30

L

lawmen, 11, 26, 34–35,
42–44
Lincoln County War,
21–23
Longabaugh, Harry
"Sundance Kid,"
31–33
Longley, Bill, 18

M

Masterson, Bat,
39–40, 44
McCarty, Henry "Billy
the Kid," 21–24
McLaury, Tom/Frank,
5–10

O

O.K. Corral, 5–10

outlaws, 11, 15–16,
17–18, 25–26,
42–44

P

Place, Etta, 33
posses, 23, 26–28, 31,
38, 42
public hangings, 38, 42

Q

quick draw, 14–15

R

the Regulators, 23
reputation, 11–14
Riley, James, 12
ruthlessness, 20–21

S

saloons, 5, 6, 12, 15,
19, 35, 36, 39
Starr, Henry, 16

T

Thompson, Ben, 21, 39
train robbery,
28–31, 33
Tunstall, John, 21–23

W

Waightman,
Red Buck, 31
Wheeler, Ben, 38
Wild Bunch, 31–33

Y

Younger, Cole, 19
Yountis, Crescent
Sam, 30